TODAY'S SUPERSTARS

Taylor Swift

By Barbara M. Linde

Gareth Stevens
Publishing

Please visit our Web site, www.garethstevens.com. For a free color catalog of all our high-quality books, call toll free 1-800-542-2595 or fax 1-877-542-2596.

Library of Congress Cataloging-in-Publication Data
Linde, Barbara M.
 Taylor Swift / Barbara M. Linde.
     p. cm. -- (Today's superstars)
 Includes bibliographical references and index.
 ISBN 978-1-4339-4002-6 (pbk.)
 ISBN 978-1-4339-4003-3 (6-pack)
 ISBN 978-1-4339-4001-9 (library binding)
 1. Swift, Taylor, 1989—Juvenile literature. 2. Women country musicians—United States—Biography—Juvenile literature. I. Title.
 ML3930.S989L56 2011
 782.421642092—dc22
 [B]

                            2010012656

First Edition

Published in 2011 by
Gareth Stevens Publishing
111 East 14th Street, Suite 349
New York, NY 10003

Copyright © 2011 Gareth Stevens Publishing

Designer: Daniel Hosek
Editor: Therese Shea

Photo credits: Cover, pp. 1, 33, 46 (top) Jason Kempin/Getty Images; p. 4 Kevork Djansezian/ Getty Images; pp. 6, 7, 9 Kevin Winter/Getty Images; pp. 8, 28 Robyn Beck/AFP/Getty Images; pp. 10, 21 Christopher Polk/Getty Images; pp. 12, 16–17, 34 Rick Diamond/Getty Images; p. 13 Frazer Harrison/Getty Images; pp. 14, 24 Jason Merritt/Getty Images; p. 15 © iStockphoto.com; p. 18 Shutterstock.com; p. 19 Mark Metcalfe/Getty Images; pp. 20, 38 Ethan Miller/Getty Images; p. 22 A. Messerschmidt/Getty Images; p. 25 Frank Micelotta/ACMA/Getty Images; p. 26 Bryan Bedder/Getty Images; p. 27 (left) Michael Buckner/Getty Images; p. 27 (right) Frederick M. Brown/ Getty Images; p. 30 Stephen Lovekin/Getty Images; p. 31 Bryan Bedder/Getty Images; p. 32 Larry Busacca/Getty Images; p. 37 CBS Photo Archive/Getty Images; pp. 40, 41 Scott Gries/Getty Images; p. 46 (bottom) Roger Kisby/Getty Images.

Printed in the United States of America

CPSIA Compliance Information: Batch #CR011011GS: For further information contact Gareth Stevens, New York, New York at 1-800-542-2595

Contents

Words in the glossary appear in **bold** type the first time they are used in the text.

"I wondered what it would be like to win a Grammy . . .

I'M GOING TO CELEBRATE FOR THE REST OF MY LIFE!"

—Taylor Swift

Taylor Swift won four Grammys at the 2010 awards.

Chapter 1

Grammys Galore!

The 52nd Grammy Awards show on January 31, 2010, was coming to a close. Music giants John Legend and Carlos Santana announced the **nominees** for one of the biggest awards of the night—Album of the Year. The TV cameras showed all five nominees: Lady Gaga, Beyoncé, the Black Eyed Peas, the Dave Matthews Band, and Taylor Swift.

As her name was announced, the live audience and millions of TV viewers saw Swift gasp in surprise. She had won! The audience cheered and clapped as Swift made her way to the stage, along with the other people who made her album *Fearless* possible. Once on stage, they smiled and hugged each other. Holding the Grammy, Swift spoke.

A Thankful Taylor

Swift said, "Oh, wow, thank you so much! I just hope you know how much this means to me . . . that we get to take this back to Nashville."

Swift thanked her parents. In the audience, her mom wiped away a tear. Then Swift said, "When we're 80 years old and we're telling the same stories over and over to our grandkids and they're so annoyed with us, this is the story we're going to be telling over and over again— that we got to win Album of the Year in 2010 at the Grammys. Thank you, thank you, thank you!"

Stevie Nicks

A Grammy Performance

Swift performed three songs at the Grammys. She first sang "Today Was a Fairytale," a song she sang in the movie *Valentine's Day*. After she finished, she introduced rock legend Stevie Nicks of the band Fleetwood Mac. The two women sang the Fleetwood Mac hit "Rhiannon." Then Swift strapped on her guitar. Nicks picked up a tambourine. They sang Swift's hit "You Belong with Me." The audience cheered and clapped. Nicks and Swift smiled and hugged at the end of the song.

The First Award

Some of the Grammys were given out before the main ceremony. They weren't shown during the Grammy Awards TV show. One of these honors was Best Female Country Vocal Performance. Swift was the winner—her first Grammy!

Swift excitedly held her Grammy and said, "This is my first Grammy, you guys! I mean, this is a Grammy!" She had been happy just to have been nominated. She couldn't believe she'd won. Her excitement was shared by all the people in the audience. Then, Swift thanked the voters and the people who helped her Grammy dreams come true.

▲ Swift's success still seems like a dream to her.

Fact File

Over 26 million people watched the 2010 Grammy Awards on TV.

▲ Swift (shown here with songwriter Liz Rose) was nominated for eight 2010 Grammys.

TRUE OR FALSE?

The first time Swift received a Grammy nomination was in 2009.

The Second and Third Grammys

The award for Best Country Song is given to songwriters. Swift and her writing partner, Liz Rose, won. The song was "White Horse" from the *Fearless* album. They hugged on stage. Rose said, "About 6 years ago, this curly headed 14-year-old walked up to me and said, 'You think you would write with me sometime?' Thankfully, I said yes!"

Swift's third award was for Best Country Album for *Fearless*. By this time, she was walking on air! The Album of the Year award gave Swift an amazing total of four Grammys!

Taylor's Reaction

Swift talked with reporters after the show. They asked if she was surprised about her awards. She said, "I wondered what it would be like to win a Grammy some day. I never actually could **fathom** that it might happen until I was walking up there winning one."

Then she said she had to leave right away. She was flying to Australia for a concert tour. A reporter asked if she would celebrate on the plane. Swift answered, "I'm going to celebrate for the rest of my life!"

All About Taylor

Name: Taylor Alison Swift

Birth Date: December 13, 1989

Birthplace: Wyomissing, Pennsylvania

Height: 5 feet 11 inches (180 cm)

Eyes: Blue   **Hair:** Blonde

Current Home: Nashville, Tennessee

Family: Parents, Scott and Andrea Swift; younger brother, Austin

"I grew up in a pretty house and I had space to run **AND I HAD THE BEST DAYS WITH YOU.**"

—Taylor Swift, "The Best Day," *Fearless*

Swift and her mother, Andrea, stand backstage at the 2010 Grammys.

Chapter 2

Small-Town Girl

Taylor Alison Swift was born in a town in Pennsylvania called Wyomissing on December 13, 1989. Wyomissing is located near the city of Reading. Her father, Scott, and her mother, Andrea, both worked in **finance**. After Taylor was born, Andrea quit her job to stay at home.

Andrea named her daughter. Taylor told *Rolling Stone* magazine, "My mom thought it was cool that if you got a business card that said 'Taylor,' you wouldn't know if it was a guy or a girl."

Taylor's brother, Austin, is 3 years younger. They got along well as children and often played together. Taylor describes her childhood as "awesome." The family is still close today.

An Awesome Childhood

Swift grew up on a Christmas tree farm. She even had a job there—she looked for bugs in the trees! She rode horses and took care of the family's cats. Some of Swift's favorite memories are of family vacations at the beach in New Jersey.

Even though she was tall, Swift wasn't good at sports, so she focused on writing and music. She sang along with songs on the radio. Swift liked to make up fairy tales. In fourth grade, she won a national poetry contest. She wrote and sang a song for her church Christmas program, too.

TRUE OR FALSE?

Wyomissing, Swift's hometown, is about 60 miles (97 km) from Philadelphia, Pennsylvania.

▼ Swift attended the 2009 CMT Music Awards with her brother, Austin.

LeAnn Rimes

Meet LeAnn Rimes

Margaret LeAnn Rimes was born in 1982 in Mississippi. She grew up in Texas. LeAnn won a song and dance contest when she was 5 years old. She appeared on a talent show called *Star Search* at age 8. She recorded her first album at age 7 and her second at age 11. LeAnn was a national star by the time she was 13!

LeAnn is the youngest artist ever to win the CMA (Country Music Association) Horizon Award. She was 15 when she won. She is also the youngest Grammy winner. LeAnn has won numerous other awards as well.

Going Country

When she was 6 years old, Taylor Swift got an album by LeAnn Rimes. Rimes is a country music singer. Like Swift, she started her career when she was very young. Swift once said, "My dream idol to meet when I was younger was LeAnn Rimes. It was so cool to see someone who was 14 years old making albums and touring."

Fact File
Swift's grandmother was an opera singer. She sang at Swift's church on Sundays.

Swift liked other female country singers, too. She listened to Shania Twain, Faith Hill, and the Dixie Chicks. Swift had many female country music role models.

▲ Swift sang during the 2009 CMT Music Awards in Nashville.

Fact File

At age 10, Taylor started singing karaoke in front of audiences at festivals and country fairs.

The Karaoke Kid

Swift knew she wanted to be a singer. She started singing **karaoke** at parties. Her friends thought she was good. She began to enter karaoke contests.

One contest at a nearby music theater was especially important to her. The winner would get to sing at a show with real country music stars. Taylor was determined to win. She sang every week until she won. It took a year and a half! She was just 11 years old when she won the chance to sing at a Charlie Daniels concert.

The National Anthem

Swift loved being on stage. Singing in karaoke contests wasn't enough for her. She wanted more. She knew the U.S. national **anthem** was sung at the beginning of sports events. Swift took every chance she could get to sing the national anthem.

When she was 11, Swift had the opportunity to sing the national anthem at a Philadelphia 76ers basketball game. It was a real thrill. Rapper Jay-Z was at the game. He gave her a high-five. Swift said, "I bragged about that for, like, a year straight."

Fact File

There were over 18,000 fans at the Philadelphia 76ers game when Swift sang the national anthem.

Cool Karaoke

The word *karaoke* comes from the Japanese words for "empty" and "orchestra." In karaoke, you sing the words to a song with recorded music. The words, or lyrics, are shown on a video screen.

Karaoke first became popular in the Philippines and Japan. Now people all over the world sing karaoke. Some people sing in their homes or at parties. Others go to karaoke clubs.

"She has a fabulous voice and stage presence. SHE REALLY DESERVES TO BE WHERE SHE IS TODAY."

—Michael Bruno of the band Honor Society

Swift's songwriting sets her apart from other young music stars today.

Chapter 3

To Nashville

How could Taylor Swift make it big in country music? She had an idea: go to the home of country music—Nashville, Tennessee! That's where country music happens. She knew others had done it. So Swift decided to do it, too.

Taylor's parents helped her record a **demo** CD of her karaoke singing. Then the family drove to Nashville. By herself, Swift walked into every record company and gave her CD to the receptionist. She said, "Hi, I'm Taylor. I'm 11, and I want a record deal. Call me."

Swift didn't get her record deal. But she learned a lot. Many people in Nashville wanted to be stars. How could Swift be **unique**? How could she stand out?

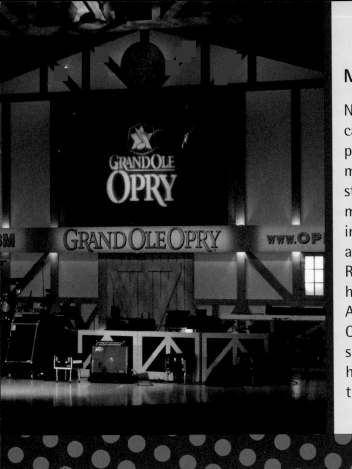

Music City

Nashville, Tennessee, is often called "Music City." It's the place to be for country music. Swift's **idols** had all started there. The big country music record companies are in Nashville. Their offices are on a street called "Music Row." Two famous concert halls are there—the Ryman Auditorium and the Grand Ole Opry. There are also many small clubs where musicians have a chance to showcase their music.

TRUE OR FALSE?

Taylor Swift decided to go to Nashville, Tennessee, after learning that Faith Hill moved there to start her career.

The Unique Taylor

One day a computer repairman came to Swift's house. First he fixed her computer. Then he taught her to play some **chords** on her twelve-string guitar. Swift practiced those chords over and over. Then she wrote her first song, "Lucky You." Now she knew how to be unique. She'd write all of her own songs!

A Girl and Her Guitar

Swift loved playing her guitar. She told *Rolling Stone* magazine, "When I picked up the guitar, I could not stop. I would literally play until my fingers bled—my mom had to tape them up, and you can imagine how popular that made me: 'Look at her fingers, so weird.'"

Swift wasn't popular in middle school. The other girls didn't like country music. They made fun of her. After school, Swift played her guitar. She wrote songs. She poured her feelings into her music.

Fact File

Taylor Swift's hair is naturally blonde. She does not color it.

This guitar was made especially for Swift.

▲ Swift auctioned one of her guitars for over $15,000 for a charity.

No Deal Yet

Swift began playing her guitar at her performances. "I played so much that I came a long way in a short period of time," she said. She also wrote more songs.

One of her early songs, "The Outside," is about the way kids at school made her feel. She was often lonely. "But then I realized if I could watch these people and write it all down, it would make a good song." She was right.

Every few months, the family traveled to Nashville. Swift kept making contacts in the music world. Still, she didn't get a music deal. The record companies thought that teens didn't listen to country music. Swift kept on trying.

Fact File

"The Outside" appeared on the *Chicks with Attitude* album released by Maybelline, a makeup company, in 2004.

First Job

When she was 13, Swift sang the national anthem at the U.S. Open tennis tournament. The entertainment director told a man named Dan Dymtrow about Swift. Dymtrow was pop star Britney Spears's business manager. After seeing a video of Swift, Dymtrow asked to become her manager.

Swift made a new demo CD of her original songs. Dymtrow took it to Nashville's major companies. The RCA record label gave her a development deal. She could record songs in their studio. It wasn't a guarantee that they would produce an album of her songs, but it was a start.

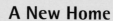

A New Home

In 2004, the Swift family moved to Hendersonville, Tennessee. They wanted to give Taylor the best chance to start her career. Hendersonville is close to Nashville. The Swift house is on Old Hickory Lake. Taylor's many awards are in her parents' living room. Her family still lives there today, although Taylor has a home in Nashville, too.

"The songs I write in 15 minutes . . .
ARE ABOUT THINGS I'VE GONE THROUGH. "

—Taylor Swift

Swift's honest songs have won her many fans of all ages.

Chapter 4

New Opportunities

Life was going pretty well for Swift. She was receiving good grades at Hendersonville High School. She was making friends, too. Swift hadn't had many friends in Pennsylvania. Abigail Anderson became her close friend. They're still best friends today.

However, things at RCA weren't going too well. The company didn't want to make an album of her songs. After all, she was only 14! They thought she should record songs by other writers. Swift didn't agree. So she left RCA and her manager.

Swift started looking for another label. Finally, Sony/ATV gave her a job. She was their youngest songwriter ever.

Songwriting Team

At Sony, Swift met songwriter Liz Rose. Rose had 20 years of experience in the music industry. Every Tuesday afternoon, the two got together to write songs. Rose said, "She's probably the finest singer-songwriter I've ever worked with. She's a genius, coming in with ideas and a melody." Swift said, "I love writing with Liz. She's a really good song editor."

Swift and Rose cowrote a song about Swift's boyfriend, Brandon. He was going away to college. She thought about things that would remind her of him. She thought of Tim McGraw, the country music artist. So Swift wrote about that. In June 2006, "Tim McGraw" became her first single—and a big hit.

▼ Rose has also written songs for Trisha Yearwood and Bonnie Raitt.

Meeting Tim and Faith

Swift performed "Tim McGraw" at the Academy of Country Music (ACM) Awards on May 15, 2007. She had never met McGraw. He and his wife, Faith Hill, were in the audience that night. After her song, Swift left the stage and introduced herself to McGraw on live television! "Hi, I'm Taylor," she said. Today, Taylor, Tim, and Faith are great friends.

A Label at Last!

Swift had a busy life. She went to school every day. In the afternoons, she wrote songs. In the evenings and on weekends, she played in clubs.

One night, she sang at the Bluebird Café in Nashville. A businessman named Scott Borchetta was impressed. He said, "Still to this day, it never hit me that Taylor was a teenager. To me, she was a hit songwriter." He invited Swift to join his brand-new label. She became an artist for Big Machine Records, her record company today.

Fact File

Swift wrote "Our Song" for her boyfriend. She sang it in her ninth-grade talent show. In 2008, the song won the Country Music Television (CMT) Best Video award.

Internet-Smart Taylor

Swift wanted people to know about her music before her album came out. She created a **profile** on a popular Web site called MySpace. She put up her biography, pictures, video clips, and her schedule. She included all of the songs from her first album.

By the time her album came out, there had been over 2 million hits on Swift's MySpace page. There were over 500,000 downloads for "Tim McGraw." Today, Swift also uses Facebook and Twitter to communicate with her fans.

The First Album

In October 2006, Swift's first album, *Taylor Swift*, came out. It climbed all the way to number one on the Billboard Country Albums chart and number five on the Billboard 200 chart. Hit singles on that album include "Teardrops on My Guitar," "Our Song," "Should've Said No," and "Picture to Burn."

By June 2008, *Taylor Swift* "went platinum," which means it had sold 1 million copies. Swift had written or cowritten every song. She was the first female country music artist ever to do this for a platinum album.

Fact File

"Our Song" stayed at number one on the Billboard Country Songs chart for 6 weeks. Swift became the youngest country artist to write and sing a number-one song.

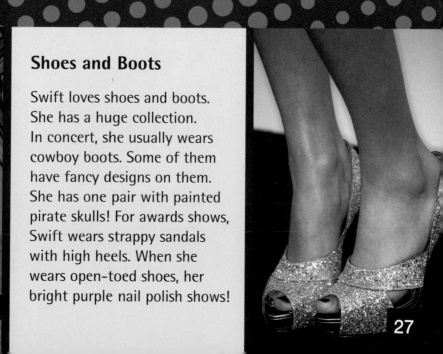

Shoes and Boots

Swift loves shoes and boots. She has a huge collection. In concert, she usually wears cowboy boots. Some of them have fancy designs on them. She has one pair with painted pirate skulls! For awards shows, Swift wears strappy sandals with high heels. When she wears open-toed shoes, her bright purple nail polish shows!

27

"She is truly one of the great MULTITALENTED PEOPLE OUT THERE NOW."

—Miley Cyrus

Miley Cyrus and Taylor Swift perform here at the 2009 Grammy Awards.

Chapter 5

It's All About the Songs

On her Web site, Taylor Swift says, "I want my fans to know—I feel the same things. I feel the same way. And my songs are where I'll never hold back."

Her fans do know this. Perhaps this is why Swift is so popular. She sounds like someone who could be a classmate or friend. Her songs tell stories about her own relationships or relationships that she imagines other young people having.

"Love Story" has a happy ending. "You Belong with Me," "Picture to Burn," "Teardrops on My Guitar," and "White Horse" talk about lost love. "Forever and Always" and "Should've Said No" tell stories about sad breakups.

Amazing Awards

By 2007, Swift was winning awards. Her first was at the CMT Music Awards. "Tim McGraw" won Breakthrough Video of the Year. That award was extra special. The fans voted for it. When she won, she said, "This is for my MySpace people and everybody who voted." She took the award on her next tour to show the fans.

She won more awards that year, including Best New Female Artist at the American Country Music Awards. When she won the Country Music Association (CMA) Horizon Award for her musical and creative growth, she said, "This has definitely been the highlight of my senior year!"

▼ Swift shows off her CMT awards on April 14, 2008.

John Mayer

Crossover Artist

Most musicians are famous for one **genre** of music, such as rock, country, or rap. A crossover artist attracts fans of different genres. It's hard to become a crossover artist, but Taylor has done it. "Teardrops on My Guitar" was a country hit first. Then the pop music fans discovered it. The video for the song has been shown on both CMT and MTV. Now some of Taylor's other songs, such as "Our Song," have become crossover hits.

Opening Act

One way for new artists to get noticed is to work as an opening act for famous musicians. Swift's first tour was with Brad Paisley in 2007. Swift told the *Los Angeles Times* that she "started screaming" when she got the news. She learned a lot about performing and traveling from Paisley. "Most importantly, he taught me that having a genuine, honest career starts with being a genuine, honest person," she said.

Swift also sang with Rascal Flatts, George Strait, and Kenny Chesney. In 2007, she opened for Tim McGraw and Faith Hill.

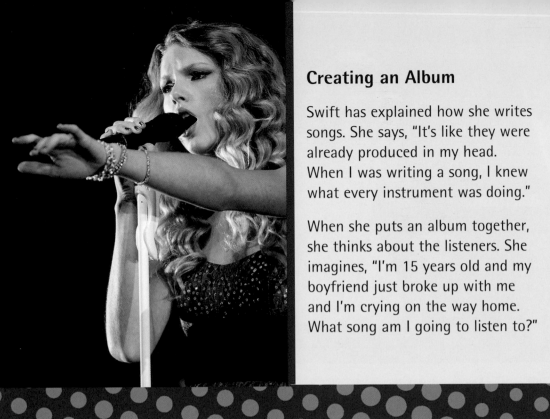

Creating an Album

Swift has explained how she writes songs. She says, "It's like they were already produced in my head. When I was writing a song, I knew what every instrument was doing."

When she puts an album together, she thinks about the listeners. She imagines, "I'm 15 years old and my boyfriend just broke up with me and I'm crying on the way home. What song am I going to listen to?"

The *Fearless* Tour

In 2009, Swift started her first headline tour. She named it after her second smash hit album, *Fearless*. On her Web site, Swift says, "To me, fearless isn't not having fears . . . I think that being fearless is having a lot of fears, but you jump anyway."

The tour covered 54 cities in the United States and Canada. All the shows sold out at lightning speed. A group called Gloriana and singer Kellie Pickler opened for Swift. She later took her tour to England, Australia, and Japan.

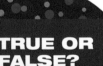

TRUE OR FALSE?

Taylor's brother, Austin, goes on the road with her all the time.

Sets and Costumes

Swift uses a lot of interesting **sets** and costumes on her tour. She designed many of them herself. There's even a fairy-tale castle. Swift dresses like Juliet from *Romeo and Juliet* in a beautiful red gown. She walks down a set of stairs in a white band uniform and hat for another song. When she sings "Love Story," she wears a white gown, and there's a church on the stage. Another time, she wears high black boots with a short, sparkly, black dress. Taylor helps her audience experience the meaning of her songs through the stage show.

▼ Swift performs here at Madison Square Garden in New York City in 2009.

"My complications come out in my songs.

ALL YOU HAVE TO DO TO BE MY FRIEND IS LIKE ME."

—Taylor Swift

Swift often makes a heart symbol with her hands during her shows.

Chapter 6

Role Model

Taylor Swift knows that kids look up to her. She has said she always thinks about the young girls and their moms. She sometimes makes choices while imagining how they'd react. Parents and grandparents appreciate Swift's efforts.

Swift told *Rolling Stone* magazine that she never drinks alcohol or smokes. "I always want to be responsible for the things I do," she says. She says there is a lot of trust between her and her parents. If she lost that trust, it would be lost forever.

Swift says sometimes it's hard to be a good role model. But she realizes that her career is more important than parties. She hopes her fans weigh their decisions, too.

From the Fans

Swift's fans come from all over the world and are many ages. Here are some things they have to say:

"I love the music in 'Love Story.' She is a good singer and also very beautiful."
— *Yeung Hee, age 35, South Korea*

"I really like her music, and I think she inspires people to be interested in music."
— *Merissa, age 15, Virginia*

"She is a good example of a confident girl. She proves that women can be strong, and she is well respected by many different people."
— *Maria, age 17, Maryland*

"Taylor Swift's songs and music videos reflect her life and have reasons to them. Taylor Swift's songs are stories."
— *Amanda, age 12, Pennsylvania*

"I love how her music is so real. When she is singing, you know you are not alone. If I were 15 again, I would look up to her as a role model. I am instead a Nana and a Gran-Nana who can point her out as one."
— *Sue, Virginia*

TRUE OR FALSE?

Swift has her own condo in Nashville, Tennessee.

Branching Out

In addition to her music, Swift has also acted. She appeared on an episode of *CSI*, one of her favorite TV shows. She was a guest host on *Saturday Night Live*. Swift has been on many talk shows. She had a role in the 2010 movie *Valentine's Day*, too.

Fashion interests Swift, too. She's started a line of inexpensive sundresses for a company called l.e.i. They look like her own clothes!

Swift has also designed a line of greeting cards for American Greetings. The cards have cute animal pictures on them.

▲ Swift played a character called Haley Jones on *CSI*.

Fact File

Swift is the youngest artist ever to win the Songwriter/Artist of the Year Award from the Nashville Songwriters Association International.

Taylor's Favorites

Clothes: Sundresses, cowboy boots

Ice Cream Flavors: Chocolate caramel and vanilla cookie dough

Color: Pink

Sport to Watch: Hockey

Sports Teams: Nashville Predators and Tennessee Titans

Tim McGraw Song: "Can't Tell Me Nothin'"

Season: Summer

Movie: *Love Actually*

Book: *To Kill a Mockingbird* by Harper Lee

Helping Others

Many of Swift's young fans read about her on the Internet. Swift is glad about that, but she also worries about Internet safety. In 2007, Swift became a spokesperson for a special program in Tennessee. She reminds kids to stay safe while on the Internet. She warns them not to chat with or give information to strangers online.

Swift donates money to the Red Cross for disaster relief. When Swift turned 18, she began exercising her right to vote. She encourages other young adults to vote, too.

▼ Swift performed at a charity concert called "Party for a Cause" in 2008.

The Next Dream

Taylor Swift turned 20 years old on December 13, 2009. She already had two megahit albums. Her first headliner concert tour was a sellout. She's received many country and pop music awards. Ryan Seacrest introduced Swift's 2010 Grammy performance. He said, "It's remarkable. You could not make up this story."

During an interview, Swift was asked about her next dream. She said, "Making my next record and hopefully it will be something I'm just as proud of."

By the Numbers

1 Number of minutes to sell out her *Fearless* show in New York City

13 Taylor's lucky number

14 Age when Taylor became the youngest-ever songwriter for Sony/ATV Publishing

17 Age when Taylor became the youngest artist to write and sing a number-one country music hit

10 million Approximate number of record albums Taylor has sold worldwide as of March 2010

20 million Approximate number of digital downloads Taylor has sold as of March 2010

Timeline

1989 Taylor Swift is born on December 13 in Wyomissing, Pennsylvania.

1999 Swift starts performing at karaoke clubs, festivals, and fairs.

2000 Swift makes her first trip to Nashville, Tennessee, to ask for a record deal.

2006 "Tim McGraw" becomes her first hit single. Her first album, *Taylor Swift*, comes out.

2007 Swift wins
the CMT
Breakthrough
Video Award for
"Tim McGraw." She also wins
the CMA Horizon Award.

2008 Swift releases *Fearless*, her
second album.

2009 Swift begins her *Fearless*
concert tour.

2010 Swift wins four Grammy
Awards.

Glossary

anthem: a song praising or declaring loyalty to a country, cause, or organization

chord: two or more musical notes sung or played together

demo: a recording meant to show off a song or musician to a record company

fathom: to understand

finance: having to do with money

genre: a type or style of music, such as country or rap

idol: someone greatly admired and loved

karaoke: a form of entertainment in which a person, accompanied by prerecorded music, sings a popular song by following words on a video screen

nominee: a person who has been suggested for an honor

profile: a short biography of a person

set: scenery for a concert, play, or movie

unique: the only one of its kind

To Find Out More

Books

Bloom, Ronny. *Taylor Swift: Unauthorized Biography*. New York, NY: Price Stern Sloan, 2009.

Hansen, Amy Gail. *Taylor Swift: Love Story*. Chicago, IL: Triumph Books, 2009.

Ryals, Lexi. *Taylor Swift: Country's Sweetheart*. New York, NY: Price Stern Sloan, 2008.

Web Sites

Big Machine Records: Taylor Swift
www.bigmachinerecords.com/taylorswift/
Read about Taylor's newest creative efforts through her record company Web site.

The OFFICIAL Taylor Swift MySpace Page
www.myspace.com/taylorswift
Find the latest news from Taylor on her official MySpace page.

Taylor Swift Official Site
www.taylorswift.com
Check out Taylor's official Web site, featuring news, tour dates, photos, videos, and Taylor's journal.

Major Awards

Academy of Country Music Awards
2008 Top New Female Vocalist
2009 Album of the Year (*Fearless*)

American Music Awards
2008 Favorite Female Artist (country)
2009 Artist of the Year; Favorite Female Artist (country); Favorite Female Artist (pop/rock); Favorite Album (country; *Fearless*); Favorite Artist (adult contemporary)

CMT Music Awards
2007 Breakthrough Video of the Year ("Tim McGraw")
2008 Female Video of the Year ("Our Song"); Video of the Year ("Our Song")
2009 Female Video of the Year ("Love Story"); Video of the Year ("Love Story")

Country Music Association
2007 Horizon Award
2009 Album of the Year (*Fearless*); Female Vocalist of the Year; Music Video of the Year ("Love Story"); Entertainer of the Year

Grammy Awards
2010 Album of the Year (*Fearless*); Best Female Country Vocal Performance ("White Horse"); Best Country Song ("White Horse"); Best Country Album (*Fearless*)

MTV Video Music
2009 Best Female Video ("You Belong with Me")

People's Choice Awards
2010 Favorite Female Artist

Teen Choice
2009 Album by Female Artist (*Fearless*); Female Artist

Source Notes

p. 4 "Taylor Swift Post-Show Interview," 52nd Annual Grammy Awards, January 31, 2010, http://www.grammy.com/videos/taylor-swift-post-show-interview.

p. 6 "Taylor Swift Post-Show Interview."

p. 7 "Pre-Telecast: Taylor Swift's First Grammy," 52nd Annual Grammy Awards, January 31, 2010, http://www.grammy.com/videos/pre-telecast-taylor-swifts-first-grammy.

p. 8 "Pre-Telecast: Taylor Swift's First Grammy."

p. 9 "Taylor Swift Post-Show Interview."

p. 10 Taylor Swift, "The Best Day," *Fearless*, Nashville, TN: Big Machine Records, 2008.

p. 11 Amy Gail Hansen, *Taylor Swift: Love Story* (Chicago, IL: Triumph Books, 2009), 8.

p. 13 "Taylor Swift Loved LeAnn Rimes," October 14, 2009, http://justjaredjr.buzznet.com/2009/10/14/taylor-swift-loved-leann-rimes/.

p. 15 Lexi Ryals, *Taylor Swift: Country's Sweetheart* (New York, NY: Price Stern Sloan, 2008), 10.

p. 16 Anne M. Raso, "Taylor Swift's Celeb Friends Tattle!" *Word Up!* February 2010, 16.

p. 17 Hansen, 14.

p. 19 Vanessa Grigoriadis, "The Very Pink, Very Perfect Life of Taylor Swift," February 19, 2009, *Rolling Stone*, http://www.rollingstone.com/news/story/26213623/the-very-pink-very-perfect-life-of-taylor-swift.

p. 20 (first paragraph) Hansen, 17. (second paragraph) Ryals, 25.

p. 22 Ryals, 40.

p. 24 Ryals, 43.

p. 25 (top) Hansen, 23. (bottom) Ryals, 50.

p. 28 Raso, 16.

p. 29 "Bio," http://www.taylorswift.com/bio (accessed January 15, 2010).

p. 30 (first paragraph) Hansen, 98. (second paragraph) Shelly Fabian, "Taylor Swift Biography," About.com: Country Music, http://countrymusic.about.com/od/taylorswift (accessed January 16, 2010).

p. 31 Randy Lewis, "Taylor Swift's Lessons Learned from Brad Paisley," *Los Angeles Times*, June 27, 2009.

p. 32 (top) "Bio." (bottom) "Bio."

p. 34 www.myspace.com/taylorswift (accessed January 15, 2010).

p. 35 Hansen, 50.

p. 39 "Taylor Swift Post-Show Interview."

True or False Answers

Page 6   True.

Page 8   False. Swift was nominated for the Best New Artist Grammy award in 2008. She didn't win that one.

Page 12   True.

Page 18   True.

Page 21   False. The job was with Abercrombie and Fitch clothing's "rising star" campaign.

Page 24   False. Swift sang two songs on an episode of *Dancing with the Stars* in 2009.

Page 32   False. Swift's mom goes on the road with her. Swift's brother and father stay at home.

Page 36   True.

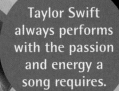

Taylor Swift always performs with the passion and energy a song requires.

Index

About the Author

Barbara Martina Linde Barbara Martina Linde is a teacher turned writer and editor. She started writing in elementary school. She'd read the first part of a book and write her own ending. Then she'd compare her version with the author's.

Barbara has written over 35 fiction and nonfiction books for children. She has also written entries for picture dictionaries and encyclopedias, and has contributed to more teacher's guides than she can count! She holds a master's degree in reading improvement from California State University, Northridge.

In her spare time, Barbara loves to travel. She's been to 33 of the United States and three continents so far and hopes to get to more places soon. She lives in Yorktown, Virginia, with her husband and lots of books.